2022

Enjoy the
Stories &
Recipes

Rosemone

A SPRIG OF ROSEMARIE

A Journey of Culinary Memories and Recipes

First published in South Africa in 2021 by Print Matters Heritage,
6 Opal Way, San Michel, Noordhoek 7979, Western Cape, South Africa
printmatters.co.za / info@printmatters.co.za
and
Rosemarie Saunders
rosemariesaunders.com

ISBN 978-0-6399378-9-2

Publisher: Robin Stuart-Clark
Editorial Panel: Rosemarie Saunders, Robin Stuart-Clark, Lisa Templeton
Photography: Rosemarie Saunders
Food Styling: Rosemarie Saunders
Recipe Testing: Rosemarie Saunders
Design: Robin Stuart-Clark
Formatting for Press: Michelle de Almeida, The Design Drawer.
Proof Reading: Vivienne Jones
Printing: Tandym Print, Cape Town

print
matters
heritage

Dedication

*This book is first and foremost
for my family who have supported my culinary journey
through numerous life challenges.*

*My loyal friends whom I could never do without –
thank you for always being there.*

*My clients, who constantly stretched me,
which led to amazing culinary heights,
new horizons and experiences –
thank you everyone.*

*This book is for you all,
but most of all my family and Nick.*

Acknowledgements

Thank you to my team of well-trained staff
who are too numerous to mention.

You know who you are
and without your loyalty and hard work
we would not all have experienced
and benefitted so much.

Cook's Notes

Spelling of certain ingredients follow international culinary standards – for example caster sugar.

Measurements:
2,5ml = ½ teaspoon
10ml -= 1 dessert spoon
15ml = 1 tablespoon

Foreword

WHEN I THINK of Rosemarie Saunders, I think of this Phoenix risen from the ashes, she's proof that big things come in small parcels and she is bright and chirpy like a little bird, and is desperately in love with anything food.

Born and brought up in the English Counties, Rosemarie studied at Hotel & Catering School which set her up for a life in food. From corporate catering, to boardroom, to any number of functions where people would say afterwards, 'Rosemarie Saunders did the food.'

Rosemarie started her journey in food in Cape Town by giving cookery lessons from her home kitchen, this, like Topsy in the night grew into a catering business, event management, food and wine tours to France, cookery books, food supplies to farm stalls, contracts to cater and teach in foreign parts of the world. Then fate stepped in and one evening her business premises burnt down. She rose with grace like a Phoenix from the ashes. And she carried on.

When I think of her now, I think of her transforming the freshest of ingredients into great food, bustling about packing platters into her car, for cocktail parties, for grand buffets in clients homes, teaching eager attendees to her Cookery Classes, training and uplifting her loyal staff.

This book is a tribute to her, her contribution to the food industry in Cape Town, her life in food and the recipes she developed over the years.

Bustle on, dear Rosemarie. No one can say your life has been dull …

Michael

Michael Olivier, Wine and Food Commentator and Broadcaster,
Johannesburg, South Africa – May 2021
michaelolivier.co.za / Twitter @manmetdiepan

Introduction

BEING BROUGHT UP in the English countryside during the 1950's by a Welsh mother and a German father, I learned early on about the importance of good fresh ingredients, being thrifty, and the value of money. Those lessons have carried me forward through many happy and challenging times.
My mother would bake whole wheat bread twice a week, gather blackberries from the hedgerows to make tarts and jam and I was often sent out into the orchard to gather the windfalls.

Coming from a family of restauranteurs it was inevitable that I would attend Hotel and Catering School. Having completed my course in Birmingham, with distinctions, I also gained a teaching qualification while working in London.

Travel has always attracted me as it awakens the senses with new experiences. Arriving in South Africa on my way to Australia in the 1970's was a magical experience. After the northern hemisphere everything is so different, the sky is so huge, there is so much space. I worked in a few 5-star hotels like the Mount Nelson in Cape Town and the Beacon Island Hotel in Plettenberg Bay, before joining Woolworths head office as catering manageress and later as a food selector, not forgetting running a restaurant on a wine farm!

I left the corporate world after six years to start a family with twin sons, followed by my daughter. Life is full of surprises and one day a phone call changed everything: I was asked to cater for some boardroom lunches at a garment factory and later at the business owner's home – and a career in catering was born; my first client remained so until I retired.

At this time I had just started giving cookery lessons from our home kitchen; little did I know how this would grow into a catering business, event management, food and wine tours to France, cookery books, food supplies to farm stalls and contracts to cater and teach in foreign parts of the world. Then fate stepped in; one evening my business premises burned down.

A sign: time to change, time to stop and reflect.

Rosemarie Saunders, Cape Town, April 2021

LEFT: Port Berry Jelly - Page 45

Contents

LEFT: Salad Niçoise - Page 51

You never know what is going to greet you when catering on location. We had set up a luncheon for 200 guests in a hangar at an airport the day before the event. The refrigerated truck was loaded and checked before we left for the night. Arriving early on the day, I was met with icicles hanging from the truck. Prising open the doors we were blasted with extremely cold air registering – 25°C deg. I climbed into the truck to see what we could salvage and thought, 'Well, they asked for a cold lunch. Now they're certainly getting one!'

When this kind of situation happened, my loyal staff would take a step back and wait quietly for a revised plan of action. Runners and drivers were dispatched to local stores to gather fresh herbs and salad ingredients.

Fortunately, it was an extremely hot, windless day and the salmon trout towers slowly thawed on the plates, while members of the team sliced the defrosting beef fillets. The table runways of plated courses slowly took form and we met the luncheon deadline.

After the lunch, the client asked, 'How did you manage to keep everything at such a cool temperature on such a hot day?' If only he'd known about the icicles.

Salmon Tower

SERVES 8

- **130g smoked salmon** or **salmon trout**.
- **400g hot smoked** or **cooked salmon**.
- Flake the salmon and pop into a food processor to carefully chop. Place into a bowl and mix with ¼ **cup snipped chives, 15ml creamed horseradish, 250g smooth cream cheese, finely chopped zest of one lemon**.
- **Squeeze the lemon juice** into a small dish.
- Sprinkle **5ml gelatine** over, leave to sponge, absorb the juice.
- Melt over hot water or 30 seconds in the microwave.
- Stir into the salmon mix.
- Season with a dash of **cayenne pepper**.
- Fold in **125ml whipped cream**.
- Spoon into **8 moulds**.
- Chill for **4 hours** or **overnight**.
- Turn out and serve on a bed of thinly sliced pickled cucumber, top each mould with a dollop of **crème fraiche**, a sliver of **smoked salmon** and ½ **a hard-boiled quail egg**.

PICKLED CUCUMBER
- **One cucumber**.
- Slice thinly.

- Mix **250ml vinegar** and **30g caster sugar** together.
- Pour over sliced cucumber and leave overnight in the fridge.
- **15ml of freshly chopped dill** or **fennel** can be added.

Taking food and wine tours to the South of France resulted in local friends joining the cookery lessons I held. This of course led to, 'My daughter is getting married; can you do the catering and organise the whole event?'

For a location wedding you are building a restaurant for one night; so it was, one glorious July evening, when a couple of hundred guests were arriving from around the world to celebrate a wedding on a gravel terrace which the family had extended for the big event.

The hired ovens had come up from Nice. My daughter had flown in to help and locals had been engaged to service the occasion. With 32 legs of lamb to slow roast, I checked the hired ovens, which tripped the power supply – faulty ovens. An urgent call was made for replacement ovens to be sent.

The next day, the hiring company arrived, swapped the ovens, and returned to Nice. I loaded the legs of lamb into the hot ovens; everything was going well, or so I thought. As soon as the party began, the music started, lights came on and the ovens went off.

Time to think on one's feet. After rapid phone calls to friends in the area to please switch on their ovens, my driver loaded his van with trays of half-roasted tapenade legs and drove around the countryside dropping off roasting trays to continue the cooking. The legs returned beautifully slow-roasted, just in time for the guest chefs to carve at their tables on the lower terrace. When the host popped into our garage kitchen to check on his Ferrari, he declared: 'Fantastic lamb, Rosemarie, never had anything like it.' If only he had known how those legs had travelled.

The following morning, while clearing up and preparing a summer lunch for 100 guests on the B list, our host arrived in the garage kitchen with a G-string he had found in the swimming pool, asking; 'Does this belong to anyone?'

'No... looks a bit small for you.' I replied cheekily.

Unknown to me this amazing wedding was featured in the Italian edition of *Vogue*, fortunately with no mention of our well-travelled legs of lamb or a lost G-string.

Lamb Tapenade
SERVES 6 – 8

THE TAPENADE

This can be stored in an airtight glass container in the fridge or make life easier and buy a jar of black olive tapenade.

- Place in a food processor and blend until smooth **250g stoned black olives, one large clove of garlic, 50g anchovy fillets, 25g capers, 60-100ml olive oil, ¼ cup freshly chopped parsley** and **milled black pepper.**

THE LAMB

- Use a **shoulder cut** or a **leg**. If using a shoulder, leave on the bone for roasting, but with a leg it is best to debone and butterfly.
- Score the lamb leg or shoulder.
- Spread the **tapenade** over the lamb, place into a roasting pan on a bed of roughly cut vegetables – **carrot, leek, celery, onion, 6 cloves of garlic** cut in half and a handful of **rosemary sprigs**.
- Leave at room temperature for **3–4 hours** before open, slow-roasting at **160°C** for **3–4 hours** or until very tender.
- Serve in slices on a bed of **couscous**.
- With the **meat juices**, add **1L of lamb stock** and simmer on a high heat to reduce the sauce by half and thicken slightly. Serve with the lamb.

FOR SUMMER PINK LEGS

- Butterfly the leg of lamb and **rub with tapenade**, place in a roasting pan on a bed of **fresh rosemary**, place into the oven at **220°C for 20 minutes**.
- Remove and **rest for 30 minutes** covered with tin foil.
- Place back in the oven for **20 minutes**.
- Leave to cool slightly before serving in slices with a roquette salad and shaved parmesan, and grilled vegetables with a pesto sauce. Delicious with the Butternut Tatin with Feta (Page 101).

When thinking of nougat, memories come flooding back of our Provençal Kitchen tours that I used to take to France in the 90's. The groups would stay at a hilltop Bastide hotel deep in the Provençal countryside. We would show off the department of the Var with trips to Roger Vergé and the truffle experience at Bruno's in Lorgues, not forgetting sampling Rosé in various vineyards.

Nougat ice cream became a favourite and I think it also had something to do with the handsome, young, charming French chef who demonstrated this ice cream with great passion in Mougins.

Be patient while making this as it's worth it.

NOUGAT is extremely popular all over the world and in France, at the weekly morning street markets, one can buy huge wedges of nougat in many flavours.

Working with problems, not against them, is the key to solutions.

Nougat Ice Cream
SERVES 6 – 8

THE PRALINE

- Take **250g Caster sugar** and **62ml water**.
- Boil to caramel on a sugar thermometer.
- Add another **62ml cold water** and bring back to the boil.
- Stir in **200g roasted chopped nuts – almonds** or **pecans**.
- Pour onto an oiled work surface and leave to cool.
- Once cold break into pieces and place into a plastic bag.
- Crush with a meat hammer or place into a food processor for a finer praline.
- You can buy praline in some specialist shops.

THE NEXT STAGE

- Whip **125ml egg whites** to firm peak on top speed using an electric whisk.
- Boil **125ml clear honey to 110°–120°C** use a sugar thermometer.

- Slowly pour the hot honey into the firm egg whites while whipping on high speed.
- Very important: let the mixture **COOL**.
- Now fold in **500ml cold whipped cream**.
- Fold in **125g cut mixed peel** and **125ml praline**.
- Pour into a cling film lined mould or teacups and freeze overnight.
- Turn out onto a serving plate and decorate with flaked roasted almonds and caramel sauce.
- If serving in a teacup do not turn out, float the caramel sauce on top of the ice cream and sprinkle with flaked roasted almonds.

SERVE WITH CARAMEL SAUCE

- Place into a saucepan **100g butter, 200g caster sugar, 125ml golden syrup** and **500ml cream**.
- Boil to **120°C**, until a deep caramel colour.
- Cool and serve.

7

Crumbed chicken breasts always go down well whatever the occasion, homemade of course. When planning the menu for the wedding of one of my twin sons, I asked what would he like for the main course. The reply was simple, crumbed chicken breasts, mashed potatoes and broccoli – of course what else could it possibly be?

Chicken with Herbs and Parmesan Crust
SERVES 6

- Bat out the breasts evenly followed by a quick dusting of seasoned flour. Then pass through beaten egg and pat on corn or breadcrumbs.
- Shallow fry in sunflower oil and serve.

Now for the DINNER PARTY VERSION with a breadcrumb, parmesan and herb topping with a dash of Martini of course.

- Place **6 chicken breasts** or 6 slices of salmon or firm white fish in an oven proof dish.
- Pour over **250ml Martini Bianco** (or white wine).
- Combine **250ml dried bread** or **corn crumbs, 50ml dried tarragon (or mixed herbs), 200ml olive oil, 80g freshly grated parmesan cheese, salt** and **pepper**.
- Divide the topping into 6 and press on top of the breasts.
- Dot **18 cherry** or **rosa tomatoes** around the dish in the Martini.
- Pop into the oven at **180°C** and bake until the crust is brown about **25–30 minutes**.

COOK'S TIPS
- Use sesame seeds instead of crumbs.
- Use only the best Parmigiano and grate it yourself.
- Serve with green and yellow pasta or courgette ribbons.

Char and Jonah were our neighbours when we bought our first house in Cape Town. There was often a sweet spicy smell that wafted over the wall. Char was baking Jonah's ginger biscuits for her Bridge tea. My twin boys would call, 'Are you there, Granny Jones?' over the wall and she would say, 'Come on round!' Instead of heading for the kitchen and the ginger biscuits they would point at the Welsh dresser and the glass jar where Char kept the peppermints. 'Why don't you want a biscuit?' Char would ask, and they replied, 'Because they're too spicy!'

Jonah's Gingers

- Cream together **60g softened butter** and **125g caster sugar** with **45ml golden syrup**.
- Slowly beat in **20ml beaten egg**.
- Stir in **180g self raising flour, 5ml bicarbonate of soda** and **5ml ground ginger** with a **pinch of salt**.
- Roll into walnut size balls and gently press flat.
- Place well apart on a buttered baking sheet.
- Bake at **160°C** for **15–20 minutes**.
- Cool on the baking tray.
- Store in an airtight container.

ROSEMARIE'S VIENNESE COOKIES

I love these Viennese cookies because the recipe is so versatile not only for cookies but also shortbread disc's sandwiched together with raspberry cream and served as a dessert with a wonderful buttery crisp texture. Cookies can be dipped in, or drizzled with, melted chocolate or sandwiched together with butter cream. A mixed box or cellophane bag of these cookies makes a delightful gift at Christmas time.

BASIC BISCUIT

Makes about 30. Oven temperature **180°C**.

- Cream together **100g room temperature butter** and **100g block margarine** with **100g caster sugar, 5ml vanilla powder** or **extract** and **15ml milk** until light and fluffy.
- Beat into the creamed mixture **125g plain flour** and **125g self raising flour**.
- Mix until a smooth soft dough has formed.
- Best to use a Kenwood Chef or Kitchen Aid with the paddle attachment.
- Butter a baking tray.
- Using a piping bag fitted with a large star tube, pipe out stars or roll dough into walnut-sized balls, gently press onto the baking sheet. Mark with a fork.
- Bake at **180°C** for **15–20 minutes**.
- Cool on the baking sheet.
- Dust cookies with icing sugar while cooling.
- Store in an airtight container.

I have been making this soup for lunch in the winter months since the 1980's and serving it cold during the summer omitting the brie. It is a one-pot soup, great to serve in teacups for a dinner party with a cheese straw balanced on the rim of the cup or a floating crouton with a thin slice of fried courgette and brie.

Courgette and Brie Soup

SERVES 6

IN A SAUCEPAN PLACE

- **350–400g sliced green courgettes**.
- **200g peeled and thinly sliced potatoes**.
- **30g butter**.
- **15ml olive oil**.
- **Salt** and **pepper**.
- **600ml water** to cover the vegetables and
  5ml chicken or vegetable stock powder.
- Bring to the boil and simmer until the
  potatoes are tender, about **20 minutes**.
- Remove from the heat and blend.
- Gently blend in **100g diced brie**.
- Reheat gently to serve hot or chill for a cold
  soup.

One evening I was helping at a fashion show at my daughter's school when a friend called to ask me for dinner. After dropping the girls at the cinema, I arrived thinking we'd be eating in the kitchen as usual. But no, I was guided into the drawing room to meet the other guests.

At the dinner table our host served coq au vin, which was delicious. The guest sitting next to me looked me up and down, and then enquired about my 'personal circumstances', to which I replied, 'None of your business.'

Not exactly the best chat-up line. Four months later he invited me to dinner and said he thought we should be an item. My reply was, 'Only if I am top of the agenda.' And so I have been ever since.

Coq au vin has a special memory for us, as I hope this recipe will for you.

I ATTENDED the Ritz cookery school in Paris for a week-long course in the 1980's. We started the week plucking the bird and by Friday the coq au vin was complete – a drawn out process in those days.

Less is more,
simple is best.

Coq au Vin
SERVES 6 – 8

- Brown **8 chicken thighs** and **8 drum sticks** in **60g butter**.
- Place in an oven proof dish.
- Saute **2 cloves crushed garlic, 250g bacon lardons** and **20–30 small, peeled button onions**, in the juices.
- Add **400g small mushrooms** and sauté.
- Sprinkle **30g plain flour** to absorb the juices. Stir.
- Add **100g tomato paste, 250ml chicken stock, 250ml red wine, 5ml fresh thyme leaves, 4 bay leaves, 5ml fresh marjoram** or **oregano, seasoning** and **60ml brandy**.
- Bring to simmering point.
- Pour over the chicken.
- Bake covered for **1½ hours** at **180°C** or simmer gently on top of the stove.
- Serve dusted with **chopped parsley**.

HEAVENLY POTATOES

- Boil **1kg potatoes** in their skins until soft. Drain and leave to cool before skinning and coarsely grating into an oven proof dish.
- Pour over **250ml cream** and **60g melted butter**, sprinkle with **salt and pepper** and bake at **180°C** for **45 minutes** or until brown and crispy.

TO PEEL BUTTON ONIONS

Plunge into boiling water for 2 minutes, drain and peel.

Crème brûlée is always a success and served in most French cafes and restaurants. At a wedding I catered for in Cape Town, part of the swimming pool had been covered to create the dance floor. I served 150 crème brûlée for the dessert. It was quite a task dusting each one twice with sugar and blow-torching.

While I was busy brûlée-ing, the speeches were made on the dance floor. The best man got a little carried away with his anecdotes and stepped backwards, plunging into the pool. He surfaced still holding his champagne glass high above his head, hauled himself out and toasted the bride and groom. He certainly was the best man despite being rather wet.

Crème Brûlée and Cream Caramel

SERVES 6

- Whisk together **4 large egg yolks, 2 large eggs** with **50g caster sugar** until pale and creamy.
- Slowly pour into the mix whisking all the time **375ml cream**.
- Stir in **10ml vanilla powder**.
- Pour into **6 × 100ml ramekins**, or even better, shallow oven proof dishes.
- Place in a bain marie in the oven **160°C** for **25–30 minutes** or until just set, cool in the oven.
- Refrigerate overnight.
- Dust the top with either **caster** or **icing sugar**. I prefer to use the latter and blow torch, then repeat until a golden crust has formed.

CREAM CARAMEL
A Greek friend of mine makes the absolute best cream caramel. Hers is a guarded recipe, but this is what works for me and remains my favourite – a light dessert that completes a meal.
- First brush a 22cm PYREX glass ring mould or 6 ramekin dishes with **melted butter** and dust with **caster sugar**.

- To make the caramel place **120g sugar** and **62ml water** in a pan and boil to caramel on a sugar thermometer.
- Add **62ml cold water** and boil.
- Carefully pour the liquid into the glass ring mould or 6 ramekins.
- Cool and chill in the fridge.
- Whisk together **375ml milk, 375ml cream, 100g caster sugar, 6 large eggs** and **5ml vanilla powder**.
- Pour carefully onto the chilled caramel and place in a bain-marie.
- Bake at **180°C** for **30–40 minutes** until set.
- Cool and place in the fridge.
- To turn out loosen the edges and flip onto plates.

Serve with **praline**! When making the caramel don't add the second **62ml of water**, stir in **100g roasted chopped nuts**, pour the praline onto a well-oiled marble surface and leave to set. Break into pieces or crush and mix with ice cream.

Bain-marie: roasting tin filled with water.

Just do it! Making your own pasta is just so satisfying, whether you have a pasta machine or not. When my daughter was at prep school, I arranged afternoon classes of pasta-making. The girls would come to our kitchens after school and make pasta to take home for dinner. We would have sheets of pasta drying on the clothes racks in the garden and driveway. Fortunately none blew away in the south-easter!

Making Pasta
SERVES 6

THE PASTA

- Simply sift **400g plain flour** onto your work surface, make a well and add **4 beaten extra-large eggs** and a **pinch of salt**.
- In circular movements with your fingertips slowly incorporate the flour to form a smooth dough and then knead it lightly to form a springy ball.
- Cover with cling film and leave to rest for **30 minutes**.
- Divide the dough into **3** or **4 pieces** and roll out evenly, or use a pasta machine.

WITHOUT A PASTA MACHINE

Roll out the dough on a floured surface and cut into strips.

USING A PASTA MACHINE

- Take each piece of dough and work it through the rollers on the thickest setting.

- Now continue to put the pasta sheets through the machine, decreasing the thickness each time. You'll need to do this six times to achieve the ideal thickness.
- Hang the sheets on a clothes horse and leave to dry for about 20 minutes. The sheets should feel flexible but not brittle.
- Once the pasta is semi dry, pass it through the tagliatelle or angel-hair setting, one sheet at a time.
- Separate each strand and hang them back on the clothes horse.

TO COOK

Plunge into boiling salted water for three to four minutes, drain well and serve. It is excellent with MY FAMOUS TOMATO SAUCE (see Page 89).

I am known in bridge circles in Monaco for my carrot cake. We lived there for almost a decade in a small, one bedroom flat of 75 square metres. There is no exaggerating the challenges of baking and cooking in our 'airline galley' kitchen. I'll leave you to imagine the dated colour scheme. It had an oven that once caught fire, burning the top of the washing machine upon which it rested. It resulted in the arrival of six burly Monégasque firemen in their fire-fighting kit and two policemen. There was no space for all of them in the kitchen, let alone the flat. The landlady then arrived to tell us we had used the oven at 'too high a temperature!'

One day we arrived home to find that the oven door had fallen onto the floor. I called the landlady and an electrician who declared that a new oven was required at our expense! 'That's Monaco for you!' I thought, 'No fixing, just replacing!' Being practical, I logged on to YouTube to look up how to fix it. Glue that could take temperatures of up to 500°C was duly ordered and arrived in the post two days later. Finally, the door was secured, but only after it had lain on our salon floor for 12 hours with a case or two of Rosé to weigh it down.

WALKING HOME from bridge one evening, a friend and I decided to stop at the Café de Paris on the Place du Casino for a glass or two of Rosé and a bite of dinner. It must have been a very thirsty walk, for as we stood to go home, we discovered the Rosé had not only gone to our heads but our legs too. We needed a chivalrous arm to guide us through the casino gardens. Nick was called, and although he had taken to his bed already, he arrived in his pyjamas.
At that hour of the morning no one noticed his attire, so we promptly finished off the bottle of Rosé and then meandered home.

Carrot and Pineapple Cake

SERVES 10–12

THE CAKE

This recipe makes one loaf tin (21cm by 11cm), one 20cm spring-form tin or 12 cupcakes. Butter the tins well before pouring in the mixture.

- Sieve into a mixing bowl **150g plain flour, 5ml baking powder, 5ml bicarbonate of soda** and **5ml cinnamon** with a good pinch of **salt**.
- Add **150g soft brown sugar**.
- Whisk together **100ml sunflower oil** and **2 large eggs**. Stir into the dry ingredients.

- Add **250ml finely grated carrots** and **half a tin drained crushed pineapple**. (As crushed pineapple comes in a 430g tin, you might as well double up the recipe.)
- If crushed pineapple is not available use drained pieces and stick blend.
- Optional add **50g roasted chopped pecans** to the mixture.
- Bake at **180°C** for **40–50 minutes** or until a skewer comes out clean. Cupcakes will take 15–20 minutes.
- Cool completely before icing.

THE CREAM CHEESE ICING

This is simply delicious.

- Sift **200g icing sugar** into a bowl.
- Gently incorporate the icing sugar with **40g soft butter** and **50g smooth cream cheese**.
- Beat well until the icing thickens.
- Spread onto the cakes and dust with nutmeg or mixed spice.

Garden weddings during the summer months were extremely popular when I had my catering business in Cape Town. I was known as The Queen of Wedding Catering. Setting up a kitchen in a garage became second nature, the marquee being erected on manicured lawns, tables being laid, and floral decorations created. Most important, reminding the host to switch off the automatic watering system but to leave the garden lights on.

At one such event all the set up went smoothly, which is not always a good sign. As the guests started to arrive, welcome trays of champagne flutes were circulated. It was then that we noticed the crystal flutes were leaking. The engraving of the glasses had created tiny holes in the flutes. At the same moment I was called into the main marquee to discover that a large candle had cracked in half and a beautifully decorated table was alight. Then, as we were dowsing the flames, the automatic watering system came on and the power supply tripped.

It was a case of doing everything twice, from decanting the drinks, to re-laying the table, to the first course of twice-baked cheese soufflé. The motto of a good caterer: keep calm and carry on.

Twice-baked Cheese Soufflé with Tomato Coulis

SERVES 10–12

- **Butter** well **10–12 teacups** or **ramekins** and sprinkle with **parmesan cheese**.
- Place a disc of greaseproof paper in the bottom of each one to ensure even unmoulding.
- Heat **500ml milk** with **half an onion studded with a clove, one bay leaf** and **6 chopped spring onions**.
- Leave to infuse for 10 minutes.
- Remove clove-studded onion and bay leaf.
- In a separate pan melt **80g butter**.
- Stir in **80g plain flour**.
- Cook out the roux on the heat.
- Slowly whisk in the warm milk, it is best to do this off the heat, keep stirring to achieve a smooth thick sauce.
- Return to the heat to cook out.
- Off the heat stir in **250g grated cheese, 5ml mustard, a little grated nutmeg, seasoning** and **6 egg yolks**.
- Whisk **6 egg whites** to firm peak and fold into the warm cheese mixture.
- Spoon the mix into the prepared ramekins or teacups.
- Place into a bain-marie (a roasting tin filled with water).
- Bake in a preheated oven **180°C** for **25 minutes**.
- Once baked and golden, the soufflées will have risen considerably, however upon removing from the oven they will sink and look quite wrinkled.
- Leave the soufflées to cool in the ramekins.
- The next day turn out the soufflées upside down onto a baking sheet and top with a little **cream** and **grated parmesan**.
- Bake at **220°C** for **15 minutes** until golden and well-risen.
- Serve with the tomato coulis (see Spinach Gnocchi Page 89) or with a mushroom sauce (see Poussins Dijonnaise Page 69).

During 2020 the world went into lockdown and international borders closed as the Coronavirus (COVID-19) pandemic spread and took hold. This meant no travelling and no celebrations, which was disappointing, as we had planned to celebrate my birthday in Italy. We stayed on at our home in Cape Town with my family close by.

For my birthday I made osso buco, risotto and tiramisu, packed the dishes up and delivered dinner to my Cape Town families. With one member of the family living up the coast in Plettenberg Bay we called a friend who is the manager of a local hotel, and asked if his chef could make up the menu for delivery using my emailed recipes. 'Delighted to!' was the reply.

On the day of my birthday in June, my family dressed in Italian colours, hung up bunting and dressed their tables, with Puccini's arias playing in the background. It was a truly festive, virtual birthday dinner party.

One cannot think well, love well, sleep well, if one has not dined well.

Osso Buco Milanese
SERVES 6

- Toss **6 good-sized pieces of veal shin** (try not to use knuckles) in **seasoned flour**.
- Seal in **100ml hot olive oil** and lay flat in an oven proof dish.
- Into the meat juices toss and cook gently, without colour, **100g sliced celery**, **100g sliced onion** and **2 plump cloves crushed garlic**.
- Add **15ml tomato paste**, one **420g can whole, peeled tomatoes, chopped, 10ml oregano, 45ml fresh lemon juice, 150ml white wine** and **150ml veal** or **chicken stock**.
- Stir well and bring to a simmer.
- Pour over the sealed veal shins, cover and place into the oven for an hour and a half, at **180°C** or until the veal is tender but not too soft.

Serve with gremolata sprinkled over the top, risotto and slices of garlic **ciabatta**.

GREMOLATA
Mix **zest of 2 lemons, 2 large crushed garlic cloves** and **half a cup freshly-chopped parsley**.

Carpe Diem for us it was 'Seize the stars!' One of the vineyards in Cotignac hosts a *Dîner en Blanc* every year, where we dine in the vineyard at long white tables under the stars. *Dîner en Blanc* is a fabulous event and has become a worldwide success especially when you complete the look with white chef's hats and panama hats. Everyone arrives dressed in white with their white picnic baskets and table settings. Panama and chef's hats abound. One year we bumped along the gravel track to the event in my vintage cream and red 2CV balancing a pavlova, white balloons filled with stars, and candles on our laps.

There is always a huge flurry to claim seats, table space and set up decorations. Having won the Best Dressed Table for a couple of years, I felt under some pressure, as other guests wandered past eying-up my layout of fairy lights, balloons and white orchids.

The saxophonist strolled among the vines serenading us. The food, wine and music flowed with notes of Kenny G drifting into the still, starlit night until the dreaded Mistral, a wind from the north-west, picked up. Balloons began popping, showering white stars over all the guests and over our snowy white pavlova. 'Everyone's a star!' I quipped, 'Tout le monde est une étoile!' The full moon shone down on our table, and our LED candles created a warm glow and, once again, we were stars too, upholding our title of Best Decorated Table.

Pavlova is the summer dessert for me. I just love the marshmallow centre, the crisp outer crust and the cream and berries. It makes me think of gathering raspberries in our garden when I was a child. This light dessert was created in 1926 by a chef who wished to recreate the puff of a tutu in honour of Anna Pavlova, the Russian *prima ballerina assoluta*, who was touring Australia and New Zealand at the time.

Pavlova

SERVES 6 – 8

- Take **125ml egg whites** at room temperature and whisk to firm peak until you can turn the bowl upside down.
- Slowly drizzle in **250g caster sugar** whisking on top speed.
- Whisk in **20ml Maizena, 10ml white vinegar** and **5ml vanilla powder**.
- Spoon onto baking paper and slightly dip the centre.
- Bake for **1½ hours** at **125°C**. Leave to cool in the oven with the door ajar.
- Peel off the paper and place onto a presentation plate.
- Whip **250ml cream** and spread into the dip.
- Scatter **500g mixed berries** on top. Chill before serving.

GREAT TO SERVE WITH A RASPBERRY OR STRAWBERRY COULIS.
This is easy to make.

- Blend **500g raspberries, 100ml Grand Marnier** or **Cointreau** and **15ml lemon juice**.

Sweet on the lips,
Heavy on the hips.

When the sirocco wind blows across the Mediterranean, one can smell and feel the humidity of North Africa. It was Grand Prix season in Monaco when I was serving a plate of Moroccan chicken kebabs on our balcony overlooking the race circuit. Above the noise of the racing cars a guest enquired about the spices I had used. I explained the mix of the dish and he promptly announced to those around him that the chicken had been flown in from Morocco. Not exactly the truth, but there you go! They say that the sirocco can affect one's hearing or perhaps it was the noise of the cars.

This easy recipe is one of my summer standbys.

Moroccan Chicken Kebabs and Tzatziki

SERVES 8–10

THE CHICKEN

- Cut **4 chicken breasts** into strips.
- Roll in **Moroccan spices**, available at most supermarkets in tins or jars.
- Lay on a baking sheet.
- Spray with **olive oil**.
- Bake in the oven at **180°C** for **15 minutes**.

I usually serve with tzatziki which complements the spices perfectly.

TZATZIKI

- **Grate one cucumber** over a sieve and leave to **drain for 30 minutes**.
- Mix grated cucumber with **2 crushed cloves of garlic**.
- **2 finely chopped spring onions**.
- **15ml mayonnaise**.
- **250ml double cream plain yoghurt**.
- Stir in **one bunch chopped peppermint**.

Travel has been a huge part of my life and education, and I'm always planning a trip somewhere. I am glad that I took those opportunities and experienced different cultures.

While working in London in the 1970's I booked a three week road trip of Scandinavia, Russia and Eastern Europe. Russia in those days was very different from today: there were huge mural paintings of Lenin on blocks of dilapidated flats, promoting the five year plan. The concept of a five year plan prompted me to write down travel destinations that I wanted to visit. Top of the list was to explore the Southern hemisphere starting with Australia in the early 1970s. The ship docked en route in Cape Town and I decided to stop off and explore. I secured a job at The Beacon Island hotel in Plettenberg Bay and that's how I ended up staying in South Africa. I did finally visit Australia 25 years later.

On the Russian trip I met a couple from Toronto, and we became friends over talk of restaurants, ingredients and chocolate. We caught up with each other in London, New York and Toronto where we tried out different restaurants and swapped culinary experiences. Years later their daughter spent six months with us in Cape Town, working in the catering business and attending my cookery lessons. She loved Italian cookery and while she made superb tomato sauces, I created chocolate ice cream! After staying with us she went to Italy where she learned to cook Italian food and speak Italian. She now owns a fabulous Italian restaurant in her hometown, Toronto.

Fail to plan, plan to fail.

Chocolate Ice Cream

SERVES 8 – 10

- Line a **750ml mould** or **8–10 small coffee cups** with cling film.
- Break **150g dark 70% chocolate** into pieces and melt in the microwave on high for one-minute. Stir gently and heat one more minute until the chocolate is smooth.
- Slowly stir **3 egg yolks** into the warm chocolate thickening the mixture.
- Whisk **3 egg whites** at room temperature to firm peak on high speed and gradually add **100g of caster sugar** whisking all the time.
- Fold into the chocolate and egg yolk mixture.
- Whip **250ml cream**.
- Fold gently into the chocolate mixture.
- Spoon into prepared moulds and freeze for 24 hours before turning out and serving with **fresh raspberries**, **berry coulis** and **thick cream**.

It's a fantastic ice cream as you just mix it, freeze it and eat it!

One Christmas Day I was catering for an international group of 40 guests who had flown their private aeroplanes into a remote game reserve for lunch – as one does. It had taken a lot of organising as the airstrip had to be extended to accommodate the fleet of light aircraft. As none of the guests were staying over, my team and I could enjoy the splendour of the luxury lodge for a night.

Being the height of summer, twig Christmas trees, adorned with lemons and oranges, were hung upside down along the length of the table from a huge ilex tree which shaded the wooden deck overlooking a waterhole. Each place was set with a pyramid serviette underneath which was a nutcracker and a selection of whole nuts, which caused much repartee and merriment.

Of course, all we needed was Father Christmas, so I arranged for the local skydiving club to circle the camp before parachuting down onto the lawn in jolly, red Santa suits. As they floated down, the sound of 'Ho ho ho' could be heard, followed by a mighty splash in the waterhole! Fortunately, there were several Father Christmases, so dry presents could still be handed out.

I designed a menu featuring as much red as possible, with chilled red belle pepper soup to start the luncheon or so I had planned. During the journey, the soup had turned and much dismay followed. Quick action was required: a search in the fridges followed and Gazpacho was produced. None of the guests knew the difference; they were too busy talking planes and comparing their nut stories!

Thinking on your feet and staying calm is the key to successful location catering.

Red Belle Pepper Soup and Gazpacho
SERVES 6 – 8

- Chop **3 large red peppers, 500g tomatoes** and **one large onion**.
- Toss in a pan with **one clove crushed garlic** and **30g butter**, cover with greaseproof paper and place on a low heat to cook without colour.
- Remove the greaseproof paper and stir in **10ml tomato paste** off the heat.
- Add **750ml vegetable stock** and stir. Return to a higher heat and **simmer** for **30 minutes**.
- Remove from the heat, cool and blend using a stick blender. The soup can be passed through a sieve for a smoother texture or served as a thicker purée.
- Serve hot or chilled with a swirl of basil pesto, or cream and snipped chives.

EASY GAZPACHO FOR 6
- Blend **700g firm, red, ripe tomatoes**, a **10cm piece of cucumber peeled** and **chopped, 2 or 3 chopped spring onions, 2 cloves garlic crushed, half a large red pepper deseeded** and **chopped, 10ml chopped basil, 60ml olive oil, 20ml cider vinegar, 10ml tomato paste, seasoning**. Check the consistency and serve with a swirl of Pesto.

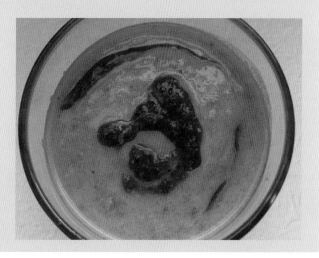

Friends are important to all of us and as we travel along life's path our longstanding friends become increasingly important to us. One of these special relationships is a Greek friend who is a great cook and she taught me about Greek cooking. This Greek lamb casserole has become a favourite, but she still makes it better than I do!

This teaches us that, although we make the same recipe, results can differ. When I used to teach classes where the participants all made the same dish, upon tasting, each dish was slightly different; all were acceptable but there would be just one or two that stood out.

Cooking is about passion and concentration. Always read the recipe twice!

The ingredients: only use the best.

The method: understand the process.

This casserole is a meal in one to serve with freshly baked pita bread.

Greek Lamb Casserole with Almonds and Feta

SERVES 6 – 8

- Place **62ml ml olive oil** and **62ml sunflower oil** in a pan on the stove.
- Sauté **1kg cubed lean lamb** until sealed, set aside.
- In the meat juices brown **20 button onions**.
- Add the sealed lamb.
- Stir in **100g tomato paste, one 450g can whole peeled tomatoes, chopped, 250ml red wine, 500g small baby potatoes, 2 cloves crushed garlic, 30ml white wine vinegar, 5ml sugar, 10ml freshly chopped oregano, seasoning**.
- Cook out for an hour or so or until the lamb is tender.

TO FINISH
- Stir in the **zest and juice of one lemon**.
- Sprinkle over the casserole. **100g roasted whole blanched almonds, 100g diced feta** and **feshly chopped oregano**.

TO PEEL BUTTON ONIONS
Plunge into boiling water for 2 minutes, drain and peel.

35

Rise above the occasion. Once a year in Cotignac, I give a cookery demonstration at our home. Twelve ladies from the International Women's Club of Provence come along to watch, sip Rosé and enjoy lunch on the terrace.

A few years ago I gave a Greek cookery class, featuring recipes and techniques learnt from my dear, longstanding Greek friend, who had guided me so well. On the eve of the lesson, we were invited to dinner with a local village friend who would be joining the class the next day.

The dessert she served was Baklava! It was too late for me to change the menu.

I complimented her, saying it was delicious, and she insisted we take a portion or two home to enjoy later. I said, 'A surprise awaits you tomorrow,' and it did, when I demonstrated my version of Baklava, which created a discussion amongst the ladies, who all compared recipes.

This is a typical Greek dessert and best enjoyed with fresh mint tea brewed with a cinnamon stick.

A little of what you fancy does you good.

Baklava

SERVES 8 – 10

- Mix **100g ground walnuts** and **100g chopped almonds, 125ml fresh white breadcrumbs, 100g caster sugar** and **10ml ground cinnamon**.
- Brush **10 sheets of phyllo pastry** with melted **butter** and lay in a 28cm oven proof dish, overlapping the sides.
- Sprinkle a layer of the nut mixture on the bottom and fold over the first two sheets.
- Brush with **melted butter** and repeat until you have finished the nut mixture.
- Finish the top with a few sheets of buttered phyllo. Chill for one hour.
- Mark portions with a knife.
- Bake at **150°C** for **1½ hours**, or until golden and well risen. Cool completely before spooning over the syrup.

THE SYRUP

- Heat together **200g caster sugar, 250ml water** and **2 cinnamon sticks cracked open**.
- Remove the cinnamon sticks before pouring the syrup over the baked baklava.

LEMON YOGHURT ICE CREAM

This is so simple to make and absolutely delicious to serve with Baklava.

- Mix together **500ml Greek yoghurt, 150g caster sugar, zest of 3 lemons finely grated** and **100ml fresh lemon juice**.
- Stir and pour into **8–10 moulds** and freeze overnight.
- Serve with a berry, apricot or granadilla (passion fruit) coulis mixed with orange juice and Cointreau or Grand Marnier.

Always, always have a stock of beef bolognaise in the freezer. I usually prepare a couple of kilos at a time so that I can produce dinner quickly if needs be. Italian dishes such as spaghetti bolognaise, lasagne and beef cannelloni, and other standby dishes like cottage pie, chili con carne and bobotie can also be magically produced.

A South African favourite, bobotie, reminds me of a project I was hired to do in Addis Ababa, catering for a series of events and banquets for African heads of state and embassy staff.

I had arranged for a ton – literally – of ingredients to be flown in, which the team and I were to turn into South African-themed dishes. I had discussed the table décor with a designer and went along to her studio in Cape Town to view some sample centrepieces.

To my dismay I was presented with a display of trainers. The designer had clearly interpreted the brief as Adidas, and not Addis Ababa. I had to explain that I was thinking more assegais and potjie pots than running shoes.

Seize the moment, eat well and healthily!

Bolognaise and Bobotie

SERVES 4 / MAKES 10 – 12 RAMEKINS

BOLOGNAISE

- In a pan cook out **500g lean beef mince**.
- Add **2 finely chopped onions** and **2 cloves of crushed garlic, 10ml oregano** and **seasoning**.
- Cook until the onions are transparent.
- Stir in **120g tomato paste, one 400g can whole, peeled, chopped tomatoes, 2 bay leaves and one beef stock cube** and **125ml water**.
- Cook out for **45 minutes** on a medium heat. Cool and freeze in containers.

BOBOTIE

- In a large pan, place **30ml sunflower oil, 2 large chopped onions, 2 cloves of crushed garlic** and sauté until soft and light brown.
- Stir in **30ml medium curry powder, seasoning, 10ml turmeric, 20ml white wine vinegar, zest and juice of one lemon**.
- Cook out for five minutes then add **750g lean beef mince** and **250ml water** with **5ml powdered beef stock**.
- Stir and cook out for **30 minutes** on a medium heat.
- Stir in **½ cup seedless raisins, 30ml mango chutney**.

- Spoon into an ovenproof dish or individual ramekins.
- Beat **2 eggs** and **200ml milk** and pour over the cooked curried mince.
- Stick **6 fresh bay leaves** into the mix and sprinkle with flaked almonds.
- Bake at **180°C** for **40 minutes** or **20 minutes for ramekins**.

Serve with yellow rice and poppadoms.

Our bridge afternoons in Provence usually start with a late lunch and Rosé or, as with my bridge partner, neat vodka. I would often make prawn chowder, which is a favourite of the players, especially during the winter months when we would play into the chilly evenings. As we played, the vodka flowed, our score increased and darkness fell. Suddenly one of the players remembered he had to be at a dinner party within the hour. Since he was my partner's driver for the evening, a final gulp of vodka was taken, and they made a hasty but staggering retreat to our darkened car park.

Within moments there was a yell; they had tumbled over a little wall surrounding the parking area and onto the gravel. As they rolled together, the head lights of an oncoming car caught them clinging together. The wall and the darkness kept their reputation intact.

Multitasking is holding your cards in one hand and a vodka in the other.

Prawn Chowder
SERVES 6 – 8

- In a pan melt **50g of butter**.
- Toss in **250g chopped onion, one clove crushed garlic, 500g peeled** and **diced potatoes** and **5ml curry powder**.
- Stir for a few minutes.
- Add **one 425g can drained sweetcorn, 600ml fish stock, 500ml milk** and **seasoning**.
- Simmer until the potatoes are soft.
- Stir in **600g shelled prawns** and **200g flaked smoked haddock or salmon**.
- Bring to simmering point.
- Stir in **½ cup chopped, fresh coriander** and **½ cup chopped parsley**.
- Correct the spice and seasoning.
- Serve with hot slices of garlic ciabatta.

There is nothing like good friends who are also cooks, as I found one evening while hosting a dinner party in our home. As the Thai curry simmered on the stove and the jasmine rice was coming to the boil, our guests arrived. I got busy chatting, of course, and forgot all about the rice, a regular occurrence in our house!

As the smell of burning rice wafted through to the balcony, I dashed to the kitchen to start again followed by one of my guests. My dear friend took over cooking another batch of rice, while I cleaned the pan and watched the curry.

Another round of drinks was poured and when we finally gathered around the table everyone loved the curry and the fragrant rice. Cooks as friends are the best to invite for dinner.

It's all in the preparation.

Red Thai Chicken Curry
SERVES 6

- Best cooked in a **wok**, pour in **62ml peanut or olive oil** on a high heat and toss in **600g sliced chicken breasts coated in 20g red curry paste**. Toss to seal.
- Stir in **3 cloves crushed garlic, 40g grated fresh ginger, one sliced onion, 250g chopped butternut or pumpkin** and **2 sticks chopped celery**.
- Stir for five minutes, lower heat to medium and add **400ml coconut milk or cream, 200ml water, one stock cube, 50g tomato paste** and **seasoning** and bring to a simmer.
- Add **one chopped red pepper** and cook out until the butternut is soft.
- Stir in **one packet of chopped fresh coriander** and serve with jasmine rice.

On occasion I have taken a quicker route with these ingredients but in a different order, leaving out the peanut oil.

- In a wok place **400ml coconut milk or cream, 200ml water, one stock cube, 50g tomato paste** and **seasoning** and bring to a simmer.
- Toss in **600g sliced chicken breasts coated in 20g red curry paste**.

- Stir in **3 cloves crushed garlic, 40g grated fresh ginger, one sliced onion, 250g chopped butternut or pumpkin** and **2 sticks chopped celery**.
- Simmer until the butternut is soft.
- Add **one chopped red pepper** and cook out.
- Stir in **one packet of chopped fresh coriander** and serve with jasmine rice.

RICE
Something I have learned: to cook rice it's best to read the instructions on the packet!

Life presents unexpected challenges, as it did one warm February evening when one of my staff had just handed me a nice, chilled flute of bubbles to enjoy after an extraordinarily successful beach party that we had catered for, the third function of that day. Guests had arrived by boat and walked up the beach guided by braziers with fires ablaze. Little did I know at the time how the rest of the night would unfold.

My phone rang just before midnight. One of my twin boys was calling. I answered thinking he was checking up on me, but the tone of his voice told me otherwise,

'Mom there's been a fire.'

'Oh no, our home… is everyone ok?'

'No mom, it's the business.' He had been driving past, seen the flames leaping into the sky, and called the fire brigade.

I hurried straight to my business premises, where I could hardly believe my eyes. Wading through the water in wellington boots, the smell was unbelievable. The kitchens looked like a stage set with melted pieces of equipment we'd used only that morning. All my recipes, the creations of a lifetime, had gone up in smoke.

I had 46 functions ahead of me that month and all the preparation had been done for a dinner the next night on a wine farm for a client flying in from Hong Kong with 40 friends. But as they say, the show must go on, and it did.

With the incredible help of suppliers, friends, my amazing staff and the support of my children, all 46 functions went ahead. To this day the Hong Kong client and other clients have no knowledge of the destruction of my kitchens and the disastrous loss of my recipe book library and 25 years of recipe development.

The dessert for the Hong Kong client was Port Berry Jelly, which needs to set overnight. I changed the menu wording to Port Berry Soup Drizzled with Crème Anglaise, and no one noticed the difference.

44

Rosé Raspberry Jelly.

Port Berry Jelly, Rosé Raspberry Jelly and Crème Anglaise

SERVES 8–10

- In a saucepan place **250ml ruby port, 100g caster sugar** and the **juice from the cherries** (below) to simmering point.
- Take off the heat and gently stir in a mixture of berries such as **one tin of pitted black cherries, 250g fresh raspberries, 250g small strawberries, 250g fresh blueberries** and **250g blackberries**. You can use 1kg frozen berries, too.
- Sprinkle **45ml powdered gelatine** over **125ml of cold water**, leave to sponge.
- Melt over hot water or place in the microwave for **20 or 30 seconds**. Make sure all the granules have dissolved before stirring into the warm fruit mix.
- Spoon into **8–10 ramekin dishes** or **champagne flutes**, ensuring the fruit is equally distributed. Once cool, pop in the fridge to set, ideally overnight, as the flavour improves with standing.
- Serve in the glasses or turn out onto individual plates and surround with a pool of crème anglaise. Serve with mini meringues and thickly whipped cream.

- In Rosé country in the south of France, I make a Rosé raspberry jelly. It is one way of making sure you enjoy more Provençal Rosé.
- Gently mix **500ml Rosé** and **500g fresh raspberries**.
- Add **20ml gelatine** sponged in **62ml cold water** and melted as above.
- Pour into moulds. Enjoy with a glass or two of Rosé.

CRÈME ANGLAISE

You can buy ready-made custard and vamp it up with vanilla seeds and brandy, or whip up your own delicious Crème Anglaise.

- Whisk until pale **8 egg yolks** and **100g caster sugar**, adding **500ml cream, 300ml milk** and **seeds from half a vanilla bean** or **2,5ml vanilla powder**.
- Blend liquids using a stick blender and thicken in a microwave in short blasts of one minute, stirring in between, until thick.
- It is best to use a stick blender to mix the custard. If the custard curdles, blend until smooth.

Majestic white villas can be seen all along the coast in the south of France, where a century ago Britons and White Russians would board trains and head south to escape their harsh winters. At one such rambling villa on a hot afternoon, we were at a luncheon party and while being introduced to the panama and sunhat guests, small talk arose: 'How did you end up down here?'

After being looked over by one guest, he replied: 'Inheritance!' rolling the 'r', and promptly turned away. I decided to circulate to find more convivial company which proved to be a challenge since almost all the guests were from a bygone era, living on dwindling inheritances. Just after a whole poached salmon was served I noticed one of the inheritors slip a rather large portion into her napkin: 'For my dog!' she announced. 'No, definitely your dinner,' I thought! 'How the mighty have fallen,' flashed through my mind.

From poached salmon to summer Asian salmon, a delicious salad for a hot day – no inheritance required!

A feast for the eyes!

Salmon Inheritance

SERVES 10

- Oven temperature: **180°C**.
- Place **1,5kg salmon** skin side down into an oven proof dish or onto a baking tray. Generously drizzle with **Martini Blanco**, season with salt and pepper.
- **Bake** in the pre heated oven for **15 minutes** or until just firm.
- Cool in the Martini.
- Serve whole on top of the salsa or flake the fish and toss into the vegetables.

THE VEGETABLE SALSA

- Cut into diamond shapes **250g of asparagus, mange tout, sweet corn, green beans**, toss together.
- Add **one cup green peas, seeds of one whole pomegranate** and **one bunch of chopped coriander**, toss through the dressing.

THE DRESSING

- Mix together **125ml roasted sesame seeds, 62ml clear honey, 125ml sunflower oil, 125ml olive oil, 125ml Martini Blanco, 30ml white balsamic vinegar, 15ml lemon juice, zest of one lemon, 62ml soy sauce, 62ml Mirin** (a sweeter version of Sake), **seasoning**.
- Sprinkle a little of the dressing over the salmon fillet.
- Sprinkle **white and black sesame seeds** over the salmon fillet.

A titled client whom I catered for during the 1980's always wanted spinach in some shape or form on her summer Sunday luncheon menus. Her home was on a beautiful coastline and when I first asked the address, her reply was, 'Drive along the coast. It is the house on the rocks by the sea.' After a little more prodding I got a better geographical location and some slightly better directions, the main one being that I had to cross the railway line on foot to get to the house on the rocks. She finished the call with, 'See you Sunday, Roger, over and out.'

With no cell phones, GPS or digital maps in those days, I set off to find the 'house on the rocks by the sea', risking my life as the trains sped by on an open crossing. I finally arrived at the house to find an ancient kitchen, a faulty oven, cold water only and the most beautiful Meissen porcelain to serve lunch on. Life's full of surprises.

MEISSEN PORCELAIN has been made near Dresden in Germany since the early 1700's. It is favoured by royalty and recognisable by the crossed swords logo. We were instructed by my client to always wash the plates carefully by hand. Fortunately, no breakages occurred during my time of serving lunch at the house on the rocks by the sea!

Spinach Roulade
SERVES 6 – 8

- In a glass bowl mix together well **400g chopped cooked spinach** (or frozen), **4 egg yolks, 40g plain flour, a dash of grated nutmeg** and a little **seasoning**.
- Place into the microwave for **3 minutes** to warm through, being careful not to heat too much. Check for lumps and smooth out.
- Whisk to firm peak **4 egg whites** and fold into the warm spinach mixture in two batches.
- Spread onto a **parchment-lined baking tray (40 × 30cm)**, well buttered and dusted with flour.
- Place into the oven at **180°C** for **15–20 minutes** until springy to the touch.

- Turn out the roulade onto greaseproof paper, roll up in the paper and leave to cool.

FILLING THE ROULADE
- Unravel the roulade and spread with **200g smooth or garlic and herb, cream cheese**.
- Lay **200g smoked salmon** on top and re-roll the roulade.
- Serve in slices with a **dill and yoghurt** sauce.
- Chop **one packet fresh dill** or **mint**.
- Mix with **250ml plain yogurt** and **100ml mayonnaise**.

A friend of mine in France makes what I think is the best Niçoise salad. She attended my cookery lessons in the 1980's and was trained in my Cape Town catering business. Years later we worked together in France developing food and wine tours for The Provençal Kitchen. She continues to cook generously and with great passion using only the best fresh ingredients which is, after all, the only way. Fresh is best!

Along the Cote d'Azur there are as many arguments about what constitutes a salad Niçoise as there are about bouillabaisse. Having lived on this coastline for some years, I have experienced many variations of this scrumptious salad. Some are amazingly delicious, not only in presentation but also in taste, with freshly seared tuna, sun ripened tomatoes, lightly boiled quail eggs and small Niçoise olives. Others sadly are disappointing with the use of tinned and bottled ingredients that have been piled onto the plate.

Mean people don't make good cooks.

Salad Niçoise

SERVES 4

- Top and tail **100g fine green beans**.
- Cook in salted boiling water for about **5 minutes** until just tender.
- Put the beans in cold water to refresh, drain and cool.
- Cook **200g baby potatoes**, drain and cool.
- Mix together **100ml olive oil, one clove crushed garlic, 6 shredded basil leaves, salt and pepper** in a bowl to make a dressing.
- Wash and dry **one butter lettuce**.
- Toss leaves in a little of the dressing to coat.
- Line a salad bowl.
- Sear a **500g fresh tuna steak**, cut into thin slices OR use **400g tinned tuna**, drained and flaked.
- Place the tuna in the centre of the bowl and surround with **100g beans, 4 ripe firm red tomatoes** cut into quarters or **200g Rosa cherry tomatoes** cut in half, **4 hard-boiled eggs, quartered** OR **12 hard boiled quail eggs** cut in half, **200g cooked baby potatoes** cut in half and **one red** or **green pepper** cut into 4cm strips.
- Top with **100g black olives** and **12 anchovy fillets**.
- Pour over the rest of the dressing.
- Sprinkle with **snipped chives**.
- Do not toss. Serve immediately.

Designer William Morris founded the Kelmscott Press in 1891, which he ran from his home at *Kelmscott Manor* in Oxfordshire and once said: 'Have nothing in your house that is not useful or beautiful.'

My mother surrounded herself with beautiful things and being an admirer of Morris fabric designs, named our family home in Staffordshire, *Kelmscott*. She often made an apple tart for Sunday lunch using windfall Bramley apples which I had to collect from the orchard. The apple tart comprised of sliced apple quarters, loads of brown sugar and a thick pastry topping.

Later in life I was introduced to the French tarte tatin, an upside-down apple tart. I make this regularly when we're in Cotignac, using Granny Smith apples or pears.

Try to find a round, 22cm, glass PYREX pie dish so you can see if apples are sticking when you turn the tart upside down.

TARTE TATIN originated in the Loire valley in France in the nineteenth century. It was the creation of two unmarried Tatin sisters who served this rustic upside-down apple tart with caramelised apples and crunchy pastry at their hotel. The tart is known in France as '*La Tarte des Demoiselles Tatin*'. Ladies, or *demoiselles* makes one think of Picasso's work, *Les Demoiselles d'Avignon*.

'PYREX' – genuine PYREX glassware with clear glass can withstand high oven temperatures and features the brand name in capital letters, whereas World Kitchen 'pyrex' branded glassware with a blue tinge and the brand in lower case letters may explode.

Apple Tarte Tatin

SERVES 4 – 6

THE APPLES

- In a large frying pan melt **125g unsalted butter**, slowly add **200g caster sugar** and stir until dissolved.
- Add **10 peeled apple halves** core-side down, and after some **8 minutes** turn each apple over and brown the domed side.
- Transfer the apples to the PYREX dish dome-side down. You may have to caramelise the syrup a little before pouring over the apples.
- Leave to cool.
- Cover with pastry and bake at **200°C** for **25 minutes** or until the pastry is golden.
- Once baked, invert the whole pie onto a warm plate.
- Best to place the serving plate on top of the pastry, and holding the PYREX dish, turn over quickly.
- Serve immediately with a sprinkling of **flaked roasted almonds** and **thick cream**.

PASTRY

- Sieve **150g plain flour** onto your work surface and rub in **100g butter** to the breadcrumb stage.
- Make a well and add **one extra large beaten egg**. Mix together to form the dough.
- Roll out the pastry and cover the cold apples, pinching the pastry around the sides of the dish.
- Bought puff pastry can also be used.

I was asked to cater for the opening of a wine cellar close to Cape Town. It was a magnificent event with not one, but two bands playing on the terraces, while guests selected their meals from several buffet stations: cascades of crayfish tails, rare roasted beef fillets and a huge chocolate dessert table complete with a chocolate fountain.

While I was checking on the buffet displays, I noticed a guest stop at the chocolate buffet, look around furtively, open her handbag and in one swoop, fill it with chocolate truffles. Then she whipped it shut and walked away nonchalantly. Hastily I rearranged the chocolate display to fill the gap.

As the evening wore on, we lit the pizza oven that had been specially built for the occasion. Guests gathered round to warm up and enjoy a slice. As I walked by, I noticed a lady with chocolate dripping from her handbag.

Live to eat well not live to eat.

Chocolate Roulade

SERVES 8–10

- Whisk on high speed **5 large egg yolks** and **250g caster sugar** until thick and pale.
- Melt **180g dark 70% chocolate** with **62ml water** for two minutes in the microwave, stir until smooth.
- Stir into the egg yolk and sugar mixture.
- Whisk **5 egg whites** to firm peak and fold into the chocolate mixture.
- Pour onto a buttered, flour-dusted baking-paper sheet **(35 × 20cm)**, smooth out and bake at **180°C** for **25 minutes**.
- Remove from the oven and pop a sheet of greaseproof paper on top followed by a dampened tea towel. Leave to cool overnight.
- Place a chopping board or tray on top of the tea towel and flip over.
- Peel away the original baking paper that is now on top, spread **250ml whipped cream** over the roulade (chocolate cream can be used too) and roll up using the baking paper. (See Chocolate Meringue Galette – Page 95.)
- Dust with **icing sugar** and decorate with **raspberries** or **strawberries**. Cut in diagonal slices.

Thhis is another of our favourite first courses, especially for vegetarian friends. We serve it regularly at our home in the south of France on hot, summer evenings with a freshly baked baguette or olive bread from our village baker. You can make this dish in half an hour!

Loving food is loving yourself.

Tomato Carpaccio with fried Capers

SERVES 6

- Slice **6 firm, ripe, red tomatoes** paper thin and arrange on individual plates.
- Drizzle with **olive oil** and sprinkle with a little salt and freshly ground mixed pepper.
- Heat a little **sunflower oil** in a frying pan.
- Spread **150g capers** onto kitchen paper to dry.
- Fry dry capers until crisp, watching they do not burn.
- Drain on kitchen paper and sprinkle over the tomato carpaccio.
- Sprinkle a little freshly **chopped parsley** over each plate.
- Vine capers and shaved parmesan are fabulous to use too.

What started as drinks for 6 ended up as dinner for 14! 'How does this happen?' you say to yourself, but it does. I thought, 'This is like when I had my restaurant on a wine farm in the Cape – people just kept pouring in!'

A friend from the village dropped by with his son and house guests, then another friend happened to be passing, so drinks became dinner on the terrace overlooking the Admiral's house.

Fortunately, we have loads of plates and cutlery so with a quick extension to the dining table and a shuffle round of chairs, everyone was seated. I just happened to have been shopping that day and had bought chicken thighs. A quick doubling of the recipe with couscous mixed with frozen peas, canned sweetcorn, masses of chopped parsley and chives, with a huge green salad and olive breads. Dinner was served.

There was no FHB (family hold back)! As the evening went on with the sun setting along the valley, we looked across the Cassole River to the Admiral's house, a typical Provençal villa that faces south towards the coast. I couldn't help wondering if our neighbours thought we had started a restaurant on our terrace too.

This is so simple hence being made at speed that evening.

Chicken with Lemons and Olives

SERVES 6 – 8

- In a large oven proof dish place **200g chopped onions** and **2 cloves of crushed garlic.**
- On top place **8 to 10 chicken thighs** skin side up.
- Pour over **375ml white wine, 125ml chicken stock, 100ml olive oil, zest** and **juice of 2 lemons, 100g black olives, 100g green olives, 20 fresh sage leaves** and **50g capers, seasoning**.
- Place into the oven uncovered at **180°C** for an **hour or more**.
- Serve with loads of **chopped parsley**.

Having lived in Monaco for many years, I came across many examples of tiramisu that certainly did not 'pick me up' or 'cheer me up' as the name implies; I guess my heels were not high enough.

One year we were seated on the terrace of a track-side hotel watching the Monaco Historic Grand Prix, a biennial event at which drivers in goggles race fabulous vintage cars around the well-known Grand Prix circuit, roaring along the shore and through the famous tunnel. Unlike the hotly contested Formula One race, it is all very sedate, with drivers waving each other past.

On the terrace, the dessert buffet was spectacular. A loaded plate of tiramisu swept past me carried by a sculpted, sequinned six-inch heeler, who tripped and landed splat in the tiramisu. Screams of 'Pick me up' were heard above the roar of the cars.

Tiramisu

SERVES 6 – 8

- Whisk together **4 egg yolks, 100g caster sugar** and **5ml vanilla powder**.
- Whisk in **500g mascarpone** and **250g smooth cottage cheese**, which will thicken the mixture.
- Stir in **50ml brandy or whisky**.
- Fold in **2 stiffly whisked egg whites**, add a little **sugar** while whisking and fold into the cheese mixture.
- Either make **sponge fingers** or buy **almond sponge fingers**. Soak the biscuits in a mixture of equal quantities of **very strong black coffee** and **brandy or whisky**.
- Layer ramekins, whisky glasses or a large glass bowl with the soaked biscuits and the creamy mixture, dusting each layer with **cocoa powder**.
- Place in the fridge over night before serving with a dusting of cocoa powder.

In the 1990's, our neighbour Granny Jones – honorary granny to my children – and I travelled together to Bangkok, where I attended a cookery course at the Oriental Hotel. To avoid a five hour taxi trip in traffic, we took a river taxi from the airport down the Chao Phraya river to the hotel. On arrival we alighted onto the hotel's pontoon and followed a wooden walkway, lined with exotic plants and arches of palms, to the cookery school.

We learned how to make chilli and curry pastes from scratch. This is quite a business, but fortunately today, a rich variety of these mixtures are readily available in food shops, which shortens preparation time.

Travel is not only the university of life, but a whole culinary journey of taste sensations, as we discovered on our trip.

Thai Chicken Salad
SERVES 6 – 8

- Bring **2L of water** and **4 chicken stock cubes** to the boil in a large pot.
- Add **8 sliced chicken breasts**, one piece at a time, to the simmering stock.
- Poach for **10 minutes**.
- Allow to cool in the stock.
- In the meantime, cut diagonally **one bunch spring onions** and **30 mange tout**, cut **one large red pepper** in strips, chop **2 packets / bunches fresh coriander**, thinly slice **one red onion** and mix together with **200ml sweet chilli sauce**.
- Drain the chicken and toss with **200ml sweet chilli sauce**, the salad mixture, and season with salt and black pepper. Serve with a rice salad.

RICE SALAD
- Use a combination of **250ml cooked wild** and **jasmine rice**. Add **lime zest** and **juice, olive oil, 125ml cooked lentils, 125ml sweetcorn kernels, 125ml chopped flat leaf parsley** and **125ml coriander**, toss and serve.

REALLY QUICK THAI CHICKEN SALAD WITH MAYONNAISE
- Take **8 sliced** and **cooked chicken breasts** as above, **200ml sweet chilli sauce, 250ml lemon mayonnaise**, and **2 packets chopped coriander**, toss together and serve.

At Hotel School we had a weekly pastry class. Our first challenge as lowly novices was to master apple tarts. Then we moved on to the traditional Normandy Tart with its filling of frangipane and apples and the aroma of Calvados.

This tart has become a great favourite of mine. It somehow takes me back to the beginning of really learning to cook, alerting the senses through taste, texture, smell, and touch.

There is something comforting about returning to the beginning and going back to basics, with no quick fixes, only pure ingredients, using tried and tested methods. It is good for the soul.

Pear and Almond Tart
SERVES 8 – 10

THE ALMOND FILLING

- Cream together **200g unsalted butter** and **200g caster sugar**.
- Slowly add **2 beaten eggs** with **30ml kirsch or brandy**.
- Fold in **100g ground almonds** or **pecan nuts** and **40g plain flour**.
- Spread the mixture onto a pastry-lined **28cm or 32cm** loose-bottomed, fluted tart tin.
- Arrange **4 peeled, halved and cored pears** dome-side up, pressing the pear halves firmly into the almond mixture.
- Bake for **10 minutes** at **200°C** and a further **20–25 minutes** at **180°C**.
- Sprinkle with **caster sugar** for the **final 10 minutes** and return to the oven. The sugar will melt and caramelise.

PEAR VARIETIES

- Packham's Triumph or Bon Chretien's firm pears are best. Ring the changes with Granny Smith apples or 250g freshly-stoned cherries.

Along the Cote d'Azur one comes across many versions of the traditional Marseilles bouillabaisse, some outstanding and some just awful. It is quite a tiresome process to make the old-fashioned way, so when I had my cookery school, I devised this recipe which became an all-time favourite in my catering business and at the restaurant that I ran on a wine farm outside Cape Town.

Fish Soup Marie Rose

SERVES 8 – 10

THE SOUP

- In a large pan add **30ml olive oil**, **one large chopped onion, 200g chopped tomato flesh**, (skin and deseed the tomatoes) **grated zest** of **one orange**.
- Cook gently without colour until the onions are transparent.
- Off the heat stir in **15ml tomato paste** and **25g plain flour**.
- Stir in **1L fish stock, 250ml white wine, the juice of one orange, one bay leaf, dash of cayenne pepper** and **a few strands of saffron, 5ml freshly chopped marjoram** and **seasoning**.
- Bring to simmering point.
- Add **1kg mixed diced fish, cod, sole, hake, salmon, sea bream, 100g shelled deveined prawns** and **125ml cream**.
- Bring to simmering point and serve sprinkled with **freshly chopped chives**.

FISH STOCK

Can be bought, however, you can make it too.

- **1kg fish bones, 30g butter, one onion peeled** and **chopped** in a pan.
- Cover with greaseproof paper and cook slowly without colour.
- Remove the paper add **2L of cold water, one bay leaf, juice of half a lemon, 250ml white wine, parsley stalks, seasoning** and **simmer** for **30 minutes**, strain and use as required.

ROUILLE

- Bouillabaisse is usually served with bowls of **Rouille** a rich spicy red pepper and garlic paste which you spread onto slices of baguette or crispy toast and float in the soup.
- Blend until smooth **2 grilled red peppers**, skinned and deseeded, **2 cloves of garlic, crushed, ¼ cup of fresh white breadcrumbs, one egg yolk, pinch of cayenne** and **saffron, zest** and **juice of one lemon, 50ml olive oil**.

At my home in Cape Town, I had two kitchens, one for our family and the other downstairs for teaching and the catering business. Twice a week I would give lessons – usually a dinner party course which the participants would rush home to prepare. The evening class would start with a glass of sherry which my daughter, in her pink dressing gown, would pour and hand out before saying good night and going off to bed. The story goes that when I wasn't looking, she would have a sip of sherry herself.

Poussins / Chicken Dijonnaise

POUSSINS, CHICKEN OR QUAILS

This meal, with an under-skin stuffing served with a mustard and mushroom sauce, was one of the popular dishes that I demonstrated in Cape Town and in France.

THE STUFFING

- Sweat off **300g finely chopped onions** in **60g butter** until soft.
- Stir in **500g mushroom puree** and cook out.
- Stir in **30ml whole grain mustard, 30ml Dijon Mustard, 60ml freshly chopped tarragon**.
- Stir in **10ml tomato puree**.
- Cook out for **10 minutes** on a low heat.
- Cool the mixture.

STUFFING THE 8 POUSSINS

- Divide the mixture into **10 portions (reserve 2 for the sauce)**. For 2 spatchcocked/butterflied chickens use ⅔ **of the stuffing**.
- Take the remaining **8 portions** lift the skin of the poussins / chicken and spread the stuffing between the flesh and the skin.
- Neaten and secure the birds.
- Place into a roasting pan and brush with **30ml olive oil**, season well.

- Place poussins into the oven at **180°C** for **35–40 minutes** to open roast or chickens for **1½ hours**.

THE SAUCE

You can make this while the poussins or chicken are cooking.

- Whisking **4 egg yolks with 30ml corn flour** over a bain-marie, slowly add **750ml warm chicken stock**.
- Keep whisking and adding the stock until a coating sauce has formed.
- Stir in the remaining onion and mushroom and mix with a dash of cream.

The sauce can be made in the microwave by warming, whisking, warming and so on until a smooth coating consistency is achieved.

Once the poussins are ready, coat with the sauce and fresh **sprigs of tarragon**.

Herbes de Provence, thyme or mixed herbs can be used in place of tarragon.

Serve with roasted wedges of sweet potato, butternut and parsnips.

Baked tomatoes with feta is good, too!

Another all-time favourite in South Africa is Tipsy Tart, it's a bit like the British sticky toffee pudding. There is something very satisfying and comforting about a mouthful of this warm moist dessert. It is not a tart at all, but actually a pudding.

Tipsy tart is one of the desserts I made while in Addis Ababa. The heads of African states who attended one of the banquets where South African fare was being showcased were so impressed that some asked me for the recipe! I think the tipsy tart reminded many of home.

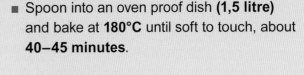
Tipsy Tart
SERVES 6 – 8

- Stir **250g pitted dates** into **250ml boiling water**, leave to **stand for 5 minutes**.
- Blend to a smooth puree.
- Stir in **5ml bicarbonate of soda**.
- Cream **125g soft butter** and **200g soft dark brown sugar** together.
- Add **2 beaten eggs** slowly, beating well after each addition.
- Fold **250g self raising flour** with a good **pinch of salt** into the creamed mixture with the pureed dates.
- Optional choice: fold in **50g chopped pecan nuts**.

- Spoon into an oven proof dish **(1,5 litre)** and bake at **180°C** until soft to touch, about **40–45 minutes**.

THE SYRUP
- Place in a pan **250g sugar, 30g butter, 250ml water, 5ml vanilla (extract or powder), 125ml brandy**.
- Bring to the boil.
- Spoon hot syrup over the hot tart as it leaves the oven.

Serve warm with whipped cream or ice cream (see page 93).

71

All along the Cote d'Azur one comes across pissaladière, which is a bit like an onion pizza, thanks to the influence of neighbouring Italy, which also lends Nice the name Nizza. It is usually served as an amuse-bouche with a glass of Rosé.

While developing recipes for the Provençal Kitchen, I took the idea and made a tart with olives, anchovies and chèvre, as my daughter loves this fresh goat's milk cheese. She is also, admittedly, better than I am at slowly cooking out the sliced onions thanks to a gap-year course at Ballymaloe cookery school in Ireland – nothing like good training!

Onion Tart with Chèvre

SERVES 6

THE PASTRY

This pastry is called pâte brisée and can be used for savoury or sweet tarts.

- On a work surface, rub together **250g plain flour** and **150g butter** to resemble breadcrumbs.
- Make a well, **add 45ml water, one egg yolk** and a **pinch of salt**, and slowly mix to form a smooth, firm dough.
- Cover and **chill for 30 minutes** to relax the dough, which results in less shrinkage when baked.
- Roll out the pastry, line a **32cm tart tin**.
- Line the pastry with tin foil.
- Fill with baking beans or place a same size cake tin on top.
- Bake for **25 minutes** at **200°C**.
- Remove the foil, beans or cake tin.
- Brush the pastry with beaten egg and **bake a further 8–10 minutes** or until the pastry case is golden and crisp.
- Cool before filling with caramelised onions.

THE ONIONS

It is so important to use a slow, low heat. I like to gently caramelise the onions to bring out the natural sweetness.

- Place into a saucepan on medium heat **2kg thinly sliced onions, 125ml olive oil, 30g caster sugar** and **seasoning**.
- Cook to golden brown, stirring from time to time and tasting for flavour and sweetness.
- Cool the onions and stir in **20ml fresh thyme leaves** before filling the tart.
- Top with slices of **garlic** or **herb chèvre**. **Feta cheese** can also be crumbled over the onions.
- Grill quickly or blow torch until the cheese is golden.
- Sprinkle with **local olives** or **sun-dried tomatoes** or **strips of anchovies,** and **fresh rosemary sprigs** or **fried crispy sage leaves**.
- As you eat this tart, picture yourself at a pavement café just beyond the flower market in Nice, sipping chilled Rosé in the shade of a parasol.

Satays always remind me of Singapore – my book Party Food was printed there. I sipped a few Singapore Slings in the Long Bar at the famous Raffles Hotel, the only place one can litter, well, drop peanut shells on the floor which are hastily swept-up! I dined on a variety of satays at the hotel. These were grilled on mini open fires in the hotel's cool courtyard surrounded by banana palms.

In the south of France, I catered for the wedding of a friend's daughter. They had spent most of their lives in Singapore and the menu we agreed upon included an Asian touch or two. They flew in their cook to make the peanut sauce, who brought all the ingredients with her including peanuts in the shell. During the preparation, the shells were blown away by the Mistral, a cold, strong wind from the north-west – no sweeping-up required.

Chicken Satays with Peanut Sauce
SERVES 8–10

MARINADE FOR THE SATAYS

- Mix **10g ground coriander, 10g turmeric, 30g finely-chopped fresh lemongrass, 15g palm sugar, 125ml tamarind juice** and **60ml peanut oil**.
- Spread over **500g / 6 chicken breasts** cut into strips.
- Thread onto wet bamboo skewers.
- Place onto a baking tray and cook at **180°C** for **15 minutes** or barbecue.

PEANUT SAUCE

- Place into a food processor **125g roasted peanuts, 10g freshly grated ginger, 15g chopped lemongrass, 75g finely-chopped onion, 6 cloves garlic, 50g palm sugar, 10g chilli powder, 2 or 3 birds eye chillies, 62ml peanut** or **sunflower oil, 500ml tamarind juice** and **5ml curry powder**.
- Blend well and pour into a pan and **simmer gently** for **30–40 minutes**.

Serve satays with desiccated coconut and chopped coriander.

In the 1980s I ate at what was then dubbed 'the greatest restaurant in the world', Jamin, Joël Robuchon's Michelin-starred restaurant in Paris. It was an unforgettable experience – and expense. It was the costliest meal I had ever eaten, but thank goodness I had booked lunch because dinner was twice the price!

The dessert was a warm chocolate tart, and every mouthful left a dark, lingering aftertaste. I just had to make it myself! Practice makes perfect, and after several attempts, I finally recreated this warm chocolate tart.

Never trust a skinny cook!

Warm chocolate Tart, Pots and Fudge

SERVES 6 – 8

Use the pastry recipe for Florentine Nutty Tart (Page 99) to line a **28cm loose-bottom flan tin**.

FILLING

- Gently heat in a saucepan **400g dark 70% chocolate** broken in pieces, **300ml cream** and **100ml milk** until melted and smooth. Stir from time to time.
- Remove from heat and carefully stir in **2 lightly beaten eggs**.
- Pour the filling into the tart base and bake at **150°C** until just set about **20–30 minutes**. Check regularly.

CHOCOLATE POTS

You can savour each spoonful of this fabulously rich, creamy chocolate dessert. The recipe makes 8–10 demitasse (small coffee cups) and will keep in the fridge for a few days. Best made the day before serving.

- Melt **350g dark 70% chocolate** broken into pieces and **100ml espresso** gently in the microwave.
- Stir in **30g soft unsalted butter** and **20ml brandy** or **whisky**, followed by **6 room temperature egg yolks**.
- Whisk to firm peak **6 egg whites** and gently fold into the chocolate mixture. The trick is to fold in a quarter of the egg whites first, then add the balance.
- Spoon into cups and chill overnight in the fridge.

CHOCOLATE FUDGE

Easy to make and wickedly sweet, the recipe makes about 40 pieces.

- Melt **60g unsalted butter** gently on the stove top.
- Add **62ml full cream milk** and **62ml cream** and bring to the boil.
- Sieve **500g caster sugar** and **30g cocoa powder** into the mix and stir on a low heat until the sugar has dissolved.
- Raise the heat and boil rapidly for **3–4 minutes** to **'soft ball'**. A sugar thermometer is ideal here. Soft ball is **115°C** or do the water test – spoon a little fudge into a glass of iced water. The mixture should set immediately.
- Stir into the mixture **2,5ml vanilla extract** and spoon the fudge into a well-buttered glass dish. Smooth the mixture and mark out the pieces. Leave to cool. Store in a sealed tin and keep under lock and key!

The Provençal Kitchen was born in the late nineties when a friend who used to work for me bought a villa in the south of France with her husband who captained super yachts. Upon visiting one spring we decided to showcase the area by introducing guests to experience the French dream of Rosé, hilltop villages and fine cuisine. To our amazement these week-long tours took off and we were able to host spring and autumn trips attracting guests from around the world.

The week was filled with touring the countryside wine tasting, lunching at terraced restaurants in the vineyards followed by cookery demonstrations by renowned chefs. Chocolate Pavé was a popular dessert shared with us, rich, creamy and satisfying.

This dessert is shaped into a 'Pavé' similar to the paving stones of many old French city streets.

Chocolate and Chestnut Pavé
SERVES 8–10

Makes: one 750g loaf tin – line with cling film.

- Place **500g chestnut puree** into a food processor and blend until smooth. Remove and keep to one side.
- Place **300g 70% dark chocolate** and **250ml cold water** into a glass bowl and melt over a bain-marie or in the microwave for **3 minutes** on medium high.
- Stir and cool completely.
- Place **200g unsalted soft butter** and **200g caster sugar** into the food processor and blend until light and creamy.

- Add the **chestnut puree**, slowly, followed by **30ml brandy**.
- Spoon into a bowl and add the cooled chocolate, fold in completely after each addition.
- Spoon into a prepared mould and leave in the fridge overnight to set.
- To serve turn out and decorate with **250ml whipped cream** piped into a ruff along the Pavé.

Fear not the phyllo pastry! It is easy to work with and deliciously crunchy to eat. I use it often for quiches, rolling up left over roasted butternut with some feta or wrapping up salmon trout with a few vegetables and baking in the oven for supper – so don't be without a roll or two in the freezer.

Fear not the phyllo pastry.
Just brush with lots of melted butter!

Smoked Salmon and Spinach Phyllo Flan

SERVES 6 – 8

- Brush **4 sheets of phyllo pastry** with melted butter.
- Layer a buttered flan tin.
- Fold and pinch the overhanging pastry into the tin.
- Brush with **melted butter**.
- Place into the bottom of the flan tin **300g roughly chopped drained wilted baby spinach**.
- Mix together in a bowl **200g chopped smoked salmon** or **salmon trout** or **cooked salmon, 4 chopped spring onions, 15ml freshly chopped dill** or **fennel, 80g grated parmesan cheese** and **seasoning**.
- Spoon mixture into the lined flan tin.
- Whip together **4 eggs** and **350ml cream**.
- Pour over the flan.
- Bake at **180°C** for **35 minutes** or until set and golden.

During a long Provençal luncheon party on the terrace of our home in Cotignac, we were enjoying a slice or two of chocolate Siena torte in the shade of the mulberry tree. We were discussing taking a drive to Italy for Andrea Bocelli's summer concert. My family adore this tenor, so I rang one of my twin sons and asked if he wanted to fly halfway around the world to join us. To my surprise he did. The other siblings did not miss out on a Bocelli concert as there was an open-air concert in our hometown the following year, and they all came.

While walking to the rustic amphitheatre Teatro del Silenzio, designed by Bocelli's architect brother in the rambling Tuscan hills, we stopped at a warm stone wall and sat down for some chilled refreshment. A bottle of Prosecco was popped and poured. As our fellow concert goers passed, there was a chorus of Cin Cin! Santé! Cheers! which was a good start to the evening. To our surprise Bocelli was joined by a famous Welsh soprano, Katherine Jenkins, and Placido Domingo, one of the legendary Three Tenors. Life is indeed full of surprises.

Chocolate Siena Torte

SERVES 6 – 8

Butter a **28cm round, fluted loose-bottomed flan** tin well and line the base with a circle of buttered, greaseproof paper.

- Cream together **125g unsalted butter** and **125g caster sugar** until light and creamy, and then beat in **3 large egg yolks**, one at a time.
- Melt **50g dark 70% chocolate** and beat in, followed by **62ml Martini Bianco, 62ml orange juice, finely chopped zest of one orange, 5ml vanilla powder** and **20ml brandy**.
- Fold in **30g cocoa powder, 100g ground almonds, 20g plain flour** and **2,5ml baking powder**.
- Whip **3 egg whites** to firm peak and slowly add **20g caster sugar**.
- Fold lightly into the mixture.
- Spoon into the lined flan tin and bake at **180°C** for **25 minutes** or until set.
- Remove from the oven and drizzle with **125ml orange juice** or **Martini Bianco.**
- Cool, remove from tin and place on a presentation plate.

TO SERVE
- Dust with sifted **icing sugar**, sprinkle with **flaked roasted almonds** and **orange zest**, and serve with a scoop of **ice cream**.

We ate this divine torte several times in Siena, in the heat and peace of the afternoon on the sloping Piazza del Campo, without witnessing the thunderous Palio di Siena, the wild biannual horse race around the piazza.

This is a great favourite of mine. It takes me back to my first introduction to Morocco when I was 14 and sent on a school educational cruise. Calling at Tangiers and Casablanca, the spicy aromas of the souk, the men walking around in djellabahs and the foreignness of it all captured my imagination. This was a time when women were rarely seen in public and we had to be covered from head to toe, no bare arms and definitely no shorts.

*After a good dinner one can forgive anyone,
even one's own relations.*

Chicken Tagine or Lamb

SERVES 4 – 6

- In a fry pan roast **5ml cumin** and **5ml coriander seeds**, cool and crush.
- Heat **62ml olive oil** and seal **4 chicken thighs** and **4 drumsticks** OR **1kg cubed lamb** – best to use leg or shoulder.
- Place into an oven proof dish.
- Add **2 chopped onions** to the chicken juices and cook until glassy.
- Stir in **3 cloves crushed garlic** and **50g grated fresh ginger**.
- Add **2 sticks of chopped celery** and **one chopped yellow pepper**.
- Add the **roasted crushed cumin** and **coriander seeds** and a **pinch of saffron**.
- Stir well.
- Add the **zest and juice of one orange, 250ml orange juice, seasoning** and **500ml chicken stock** or to cover.
- Bring to the boil and pour over the sealed chicken.
- Cook on top of the stove or in the oven **160°C** until the chicken is tender – about **1 hour**.
- Stir in **150g soaked pitted apricot halves, and 5ml honey**.
- Serve with lots of **chopped coriander** and **couscous**.

One of my sons loves this pecan tart and over the years we have refined and reworked the recipe a few times, to achieve a result that satisfies and lingers. The pastry has to be buttery and crisp, the filling nutty and moist. After many bake-offs and tastings, my son declared, 'This one's the best!'

Practice makes perfect!

Pecan Tart

SERVES 6 – 8

THE PASTRY

Makes: one 24cm loose-bottom, fluted flan tin. Making your own pastry is a skill worth mastering and always best, so here we go:

- Onto a work surface sift **170g plain flour, 30g icing sugar**.
- Make a well and add **100g soft butter**.
- Rub into the breadcrumb stage.
- Make a well and add **one large beaten egg** and a good pinch of **vanilla powder**.
- Combine to form the dough.
- Roll out to fit a well-buttered **24cm loose-bottom, fluted flan tin**.
- Chill for **30 minutes** in the fridge.
- Line the pastry with **tin foil** and place a cake tin on top or use baking beans.
- Place into the oven at **180°C** for **25 minutes**.
- Remove the cake tin and foil and place back into the oven.
- Watch carefully for **5–8 minutes** as the crust browns up, not too much though.
- Cool before spooning in the filling.

THE FILLING

- In a glass bowl place **100g butter, 50g golden syrup, 40g soft brown sugar**.
- **Microwave on high for 2–3 minutes** until the ingredients are combined.
- Stir well and cool completely.
- Stir **2 beaten eggs** into the cooled mix.
- Stir in **100g roughly chopped pecans, 25g plain flour** and **25g self-raising flour**.
- Spread onto the pastry base.
- Sprinkle a few chopped pecans on top.
- Bake at **160°C** for **20–25 minutes** or until the filling has just set.
- Cool and serve in slices with thick cream.

Company team-building cooking classes were as popular as my Men in the Kitchen courses I held in the 1990's. On one occasion, an IT company asked for an Italian cooking lesson in which everyone could participate. In a large kitchen space this is fine, but the boss had a small, smart kitchen in his Victorian home. Here we were to hold the cook-off before taking the results to their offices so the team could show off their morning's efforts for lunch.

Preparing and cooking has to be taken seriously, but the boss-man was so busy joking and larking about that his spinach and ricotta gnocchi ended up as spinach soup! A quick menu change was called for, or so he thought.

Fortunately I had anticipated the soup catastrophe and, as one learns as a Brownie: 'Be prepared!' And I was ... with back-up: reserve stock that I had made the day before. The menu didn't change and the Boss didn't lose face. Over lunch he smiled and winked cheekily at me across the table.

GNOCCHI is really a dumpling and it varies, made from potato or semolina, vegetables with herbs and ricotta, depending on the region of Italy.

Spinach and Ricotta Gnocchi

SERVES 6

- In a deep frying pan melt **60g butter**, add **300g chopped cooked spinach** and cook until quite dry.
- Take off the heat and stir in **250g ricotta, 45g plain flour** and **2 beaten eggs**.
- Return to the heat and gently cook through for **3 minutes**.
- Remove from the heat and stir in **40g parmesan** and **seasoning**.
- Leave the mixture to **cool completely**.
- Shape into **16–18 balls**.
- Pop in the fridge overnight.
- Poach in salted simmering water for **6–7 minutes**. Serve with my famous tomato sauce.

TOMATO SAUCE

- Place in a glass bowl **2 large sliced onions, 2 cloves of crushed garlic** and **30ml olive oil**. Cover and microwave for **4 minutes** on high.
- Add **one 450g canned whole peeled tomatoes chopped, 120g tomato paste, 10ml honey, 10ml dried marjoram** and **seasoning**.
- Microwave for **4 minutes**.
- Stick blend until smooth.

Dinner in 20 minutes? Yes, it is possible!

My family love risotto, and one evening while living in Monaco, we were gathered in our tiny flat and ready for dinner: prawn risotto was the answer.

My daughter and I headed for the galley kitchen while the men laid the table on the balcony and poured glasses of a crisp, chilled Rosé. Out came the wok and we followed our tried and tested recipe.

Prawn Risotto
SERVES 6

- In a wok place **60ml olive oil** with **2 chopped onions** and **2 cloves crushed garlic**.
- Cook slowly, before adding the **zest** and **juice of one lemon**, and **125ml Martini Bianco** or **white wine**, and stir well.
- Add **400g Arborio rice**. Stir, and stir again, to soak up the flavours.
- With **1L vegetable stock** gradually ladle enough stock to just cover the rice. Let it cook out, and then add more stock, stirring each time. This should take about **15 minutes** until the rice is just cooked.
- Stir in **500g shelled raw prawns** and heat through.
- Stir in **125g grated parmesan**.
- Serve with **chopped chives, fennel** or **dill**.
- Instead of prawns you can also stir in **300g sliced mushrooms**. Use porcini mushrooms for the best flavour.

TURN LEFTOVER RISOTTO INTO DELICIOUS SUPPLI BALLS.

- Take **one cup of risotto**, mix in **one egg** and **50g grated parmesan**, shape into balls around bocconcini (small balls of mozzarella). Chill, roll in **dried breadcrumbs**, then shallow or deep fry.

Rice was brought to Italy directly from the Orient by Venetian ships during the Crusades, but only became embedded in Italian cooking in the mid-sixteenth century. The best types of rice for risotto are grown near Novara in Piedmont. Rice is generally divided into three categories in Italy: Conune, Semifino and Fino. Fino, such as the short-grained Arborio rice grown in the Po Valley of northern Italy, is best for risotto because it absorbs the liquid while retaining its shape. The high starch content of Arborio lends a fabulous creaminess to risotto. Other types of risotto rice are Vialone and Carnaroli.

When we were living in Monaco, I played bridge with a whole host of different people, one of whom lived in a villa overlooking the Principality. One day I was asked if I would give a cookery demonstration to a group of her friends followed by lunch and naturally a glass or two of Rosé.

The white high-tech kitchen was concealed behind wide sliding doors which opened onto the dining room and terrace by an eye-shaped pool. As I cooked the lunch the guests chatted, laid the table with linen, china, and glassware, all of which was embossed in gold. As I made the ice cream I quipped, 'This dessert is stirred but not shaken.'

Ice Cream
SERVES 6 – 8

- Whip **4 egg yolks** and **200g caster sugar** until very thick.
- Fold in **500ml fruit purée**, such as mango, strawberry, raspberry.
- Fold in **250ml whipped cream**.
- Pour into one large mould lined with cling film or **8** individual moulds.
- Place into the **freezer** for **8 hours**.
- Turn out and serve with a **berry coulis** and sprinkle with **flaked roasted almonds**.

SERVE WITH BERRY COULIS
- Place into a bowl.
- **500g raspberries** or **strawberries**.
- Add **100ml Grand Marnier**.
- Squeeze of **fresh lemon juice**.
- Using a stick blender purée until smooth.

I often made this galette as a wedding cake since it could take the place of dessert. One hot afternoon a tiered chocolate meringue galette was en route to a prestigious hotel as a wedding cake. My student driver had to brake suddenly sending the top half of the galette sliding across the boot of the car. She arrived back at our kitchens in tears with the galette in melted pieces. 'Oh dear,' I said, 'Don't worry, take this one!' This was a galette for another wedding the next day.

I reassembled the damaged galette with lashings of chocolate cream and our client never knew the journey their wedding cake had taken. Everyone was happy, except my family who were hoping to enjoy the damaged galette.

The moral is, of course, to always have a spare to hand!

*Little steps,
big results.*

Chocolate Meringue Galette

SERVES 8 – 10

- Take **250ml egg whites** at room temperature.
- Whisk to a firm peak using an electric whisk on high speed.
- Slowly, slowly add **500g caster sugar** in a waterfall, whisking all the time.
- By hand, using the whisk, gently fold in **60g sifted cocoa powder**.
- Divide the mixture into two and spoon onto two baking trays lined with baking or parchment paper.
- From the centre of the meringue mass, gently spread it into a circle about 20cm in circumference.
- Bake for **1½–2 hours** at **110°C** or until the meringue disc peels away from the paper.
- Cool in the oven with the door open.

THE CHOCOLATE CREAM
- Place **250g dark 70% chocolate** into a glass bowl with **125ml water**.
- Melt over a bain-marie or gently in the microwave.
- Stir until smooth.
- Cool completely.
- Lightly whip **500ml cream** until thick and ribbon like, then carefully fold in the chocolate mixture.

- Sandwich the meringues together with ⅓ of the chocolate cream.
- Completely cover the galette with the remaining chocolate cream.
- Sprinkle **chocolate shavings** over the galette and **dust with icing sugar** or drizzle with **melted chocolate**.
- Chill well before serving.
- Serve in slices – dip a knife into hot water, quickly dry and slide the hot blade through the galette.

Salad *chèvre chaud* is the first dish my daughter likes to eat on arrival at our home in Cotignac, France. It's a quick walk down to the village to find this salad at one of the pavement cafes shaded by plane trees on the Cours Gambetta. Essentially cheese on toast with salad, it's best enjoyed with a glass of Rosé, of course which we drink like cordial in the Var, true Rosé country.

Most French villages and towns have squares or streets named after statesmen or famous people. Leon Gambetta, from whom the Cours Gambetta takes its name, was a statesman in the 1800's. Famed author Victor Hugo has also lent his name to many a street across France. It was while in exile in Guernsey that he wrote *Les Misérables.* He installed his mistress in the house next door and raised a white flag when his wife went out to indicate that the coast was clear!

A day without wine is like a day without sunshine.

Salad Chèvre Chaud

- Fry **sliced baguette** on one side in a little **oil**.
- Place on a baking sheet fried-side down, top with a slice of *chèvre* and grill or blow torch until brown.

- Arrange on **butter lettuce leaves** tossed in a **vinaigrette** and serve.
- Plump up the salad with **tomato** wedges, a dusting of **snipped chives, black olives** and **thinly sliced red onion**.

I came across Florentine tarts in 1989 while wandering through the ancient streets and alleys of Florence. The magnificent Duomo Santa Maria del Fiore appeared in front of me with the rich smell of espresso, roasting nuts, and caramel tempting me to stop and sit at a pavement café for a slice of nutty tart and a coffee.

At home, I got to work to recreate the nutty tart to share with the groups of ladies that attended my weekly cookery classes at my home. The tart became a favourite for the catering business, too, served as a selection of Italian tortes.

WHILE ENJOYING a slice, close your eyes and think of the streets of Florence, the piazzas, the Ponte Vecchio and the Uffizi gallery and Botticelli's Birth of Venus.

Live. Love. Cook.

Florentine Nutty Tart
SERVES 8–10

Makes: one 32cm loose-bottomed fluted flan tin.

MAKING THE PASTRY

We all know you can buy pastry, but there is something special about making your own pastry, working with your hands to form a soft, pliable dough.

- Sift **200g plain flour** and **50g icing sugar** onto your work surface.
- Make a well and add **160g unsalted butter** at room-temperature, **3 or 4 egg yolks** and a **pinch of vanilla powder** in the centre of the well.
- Gradually bring the ingredients together using your fingertips, working it into a smooth dough, being careful not to over work it.
- Roll the pastry out and line a buttered flan tin, place in the **fridge** for **30 minutes**.
- Line the chilled pastry with tin foil, top with dried beans or a cake tin.
- Bake at **200°C** for **20 minutes**.

- Remove the beans or cake tin and foil.
- Place the pastry shell back in the oven at **180°C** for **15–20 minute**s to turn golden, watch carefully.
- Once baked leave to cool.

THE CARAMEL

- Place **100g unsalted butter, 200g caster sugar, 125ml of golden syrup** and **250ml cream** into a thick bottomed saucepan and bring it to the boil.
- Boil to a caramel colour on a **medium heat** for **10–15 minutes** until 'soft ball' has been reached on a sugar thermometer or spoon a droplet into cold water – It should form a soft ball.
- Stir in **62ml cream** followed by **300g roasted nuts** (flaked almonds, pecans, or walnuts).
- Pour immediately into the baked flan case. Leave to cool completely before serving in slices.

After my business premises went up in smoke in February 2001, one of my suppliers offered me space in her floristry warehouse for my weekly cookery classes. One of the first dishes I made there was butternut tart.

My supplier's staff loved the cooking smells that wafted, mingling with the scent of the floral pieces they were creating. At midday, however, there was only one aroma that pulled us all together, the smell of lunch.

You are what you eat.

Butternut Soup, Butternut Tatin and Tomato Tatin

SERVES 4

BUTTERNUT TART

- Peel and slice **1kg butternut**.
- Sauté in **50ml olive oil** and **30g butter** until evenly brown.
- Season well and arrange in an oven proof dish. I like to use a **22cm round** PYREX pie dish. Leave to cool.
- Make the pastry by gently rubbing together **150g plain flour** and **100g room-temperature butter** to the breadcrumb stage. Make a well in the middle.
- Add **one egg** and **30ml water**. Pull the dough together and roll out to fit the pie dish.
- Pinch the sides of the pastry around the edge of the dish and bake at **180°C** for **30 minutes**.
- Once the pastry is golden, invert the dish to serve the tart upside down as you would a tarte tatin. Sprinkle with **crumbled feta cheese** to serve.

BUTTERNUT SOUP

- Take **1kg peeled and diced butternut, 2 chopped onions, 2 vegetable stock cubes, 1L water, 15ml olive oil,** and **salt and pepper**. Place all the ingredients into a saucepan, bring to the boil and simmer until the butternut is tender. Cool before blending. Serve with **chopped coriander**.

CURRIED BUTTERNUT SOUP

- This is delicious! To turn butternut soup into a curried version, simply place the **oil** and **onions** in a saucepan and sweat until transparent and soft. Then stir in **10ml curry powder** and cook out for a couple of minutes. Add the butternut soup ingredients, cook and serve as above. If the soup tastes a litter bitter, stir in some sugar or clear honey. Sherry can be stirred into the soup just before serving.

ROASTED BUTTERNUT

- Simply cut the **butternut** (skin on or peeled) into wedges, deseed, and dust with **salt, pepper** and **cinnamon**. Drizzle with **olive oil** and open roast in the oven for **40 minutes** at **180°C** or until soft. Serve as a side dish.
- **Ring the changes** with 8 ripe red tomatoes cut in half horizontally, season generously, place in a fry pan, cut side down, with **100g of sizzling butter**; seal quickly, then turn over to brown the domed side. Be careful NOT to overcook only SEAL. Place into a PYREX pie dish dome side down, top with **2 sliced browned** and **softened onions**, cool, then cover with pastry as for a tatin and bake as above. Turn out and serve with sprinkled **roasted pinenuts** and drizzled with **basil pesto**.

Chicken Quenelles were always a big hit with guests on my Provençal Kitchen cooking tours of France, who could not get enough of them.

A quenelle is a dumpling and originated with fish, in fact pike. Since pike is such a bony fish, the flesh is removed and mixed with eggs, then pounded before being seasoned, shaped into ovals, and poached, a bit like spinach gnocchi.

I have chosen to use chicken with chives and mace. It is best served over tender homemade tagliatelle with a sprinkling of parmesan.

Chicken Quenelles with Champagne Sauce and Tagliatelle

SERVES 6 – 8

- Pound **1kg chicken breast** in a food processor.
- Stir in **½ cup snipped chives, 125ml crème fraîche, seasoning, 10ml ground mace** (the amber outer coating of nutmeg) or **nutmeg, 4 egg yolks** and **60ml fresh white breadcrumbs**.
- Fold in **2 egg whites**, stiffly whipped.
- Shape into golf size balls.
- Bring **1L chicken stock** to simmering point, add the chicken balls and poach for five minutes.
- Remove and arrange on cooked tagliatelle.

THE SAUCE
- Whisk **6 egg yolks, 250ml cream** and **20ml corn flour** over a bain-marie, slowly adding **500ml champagne** or **sparkling white wine**. As the sauce heats up, so it will thicken.
- Stir in **60ml snipped chives**.

FRIED BREADCRUMBS
- Melt **60g butter** in a frying pan and fry **250ml fresh white breadcrumbs** until crisp and golden.

TO SERVE
Coat the chicken balls with the sauce and dust with fried breadcrumbs and a sprinkling of parmesan.

Notes

Notes

Notes